W9-BKG-871

A Day with a Librarian

By Jan Kottke

Children's Press
A Division of Grolier Publishing
New York / London / Hong Kong / Sydney
Danbury, Connecticut

Special thanks to the faculty and student body at the Bellport Middle School
Photo Credits: All photos by Thaddeus Harden
Contributing Editor: Jennifer Ceaser
Book Design: Michael DeLisio

Visit Children's Press on the Internet at:
http://publishing.grolier.com

Library of Congress Cataloging-in-Publication Data

Kottke, Jan.
    A day with a librarian / by Jan Kottke.
      p. cm. — (Hard work)
    Includes bibliographical references and index.
    Summary: Explains in simple terms some of the duties of a librarian.
    ISBN 0-516-23089-1 (lib. bdg.) — ISBN 0-516-23014-X (pbk.)
    1. Librarians—Juvenile literature. 2.Libraries—Juvenile literature. [1. Librarians. 2.
Occupations.] I. Title.

Z682.K68 2000
020'.92—dc21

                                                                    00-024585

Contents

My name is Mrs. Napolitano.

I work at the **library**.

I am a **librarian**.

5

I help people find what they need in the library.

I help people find the answers to their questions.

7

Chris wants a certain book.

I show him how to find it in the **catalog.**

A catalog is a list of books.

9

Ryan is doing a report for school.

He needs to find the right **magazine.**

I show him where to look.

11

Brianna is having trouble with the computer.

I teach her how to use it.

Pascale is looking for a **video**.

I show her where to find it.

I also check out books to people.

I **stamp** a date on a card.

It tells people when the book is **due**.

Every day books are **returned** to the library.

I put each book back on the **bookshelf**.

A librarian has a busy job.

I am never too busy to answer a question.

I am always here to help.

21

New Words

bookshelf (**buk**-shelf) a thin piece of wood or metal that holds books

catalog (**kat**-uh-log) a list of library books on a computer

due (**do**) needed back

librarian (ly-**brer**-ee-n) a person who works at a library

library (**ly**-brer-ee) a building where items such as books and videos can be borrowed

magazine (mag-eh-**zeen**) something that has news, stories, and pictures

returned (ree-**turnd**) given back

stamp (**stamp**) mark something using ink

video (**vid**-ee-oh) a movie or TV show that has been taped

To Find Out More

Books
Information, Please: The Librarian
by Patricia Lakin
Raintree/Steck-Vaughn

Librarians
by Dee Ready
Capstone Press

Library Lil
by Suzanne Williams
Penguin Putnam

Ms. Davison, Our Librarian
by Alice K. Flanagan
Children's Press

Web Site
ICONnect—Kids Connect
http://www.ala.org/ICONN/kidsconn.html
On this site, you can ask a librarian a question and get an answer in two days.

23

Index

About the Author
Jan Kottke is the owner/director of several preschools in the Tidewater area of Virginia. A lifelong early education professional, she is completing a phonics reading series for preschoolers.

Reading Consultants
Kris Flynn, Coordinator, Small School District Literacy, The San Diego County Office of Education

Shelly Forys, Certified Reading Recovery Specialist, W.J. Zahnow Elementary School, Waterloo, IL

Peggy McNamara, Professor, Bank Street College of Education, Reading and Literacy Program

24